Spooky Action at a Distance

SPOOKY
ACTION
at a DISTANCE

double-title poems by
David Alpaugh

WORD GALAXY PRESS
An imprint of Able Muse Press

Word Galaxy Press

www.wordgalaxy.com

Printed in the United States of America

Library of Congress Control Number: 2019956622

ISBN 978-1-77349-051-9 (paperback)
ISBN 978-1-77349-052-6 (digital)

Cover image: "That Far" by Juskteez Vu

Cover & book design by Alexander Pepple

Word Galaxy Press is an imprint of Able Muse Press—at
www.ablemusepress.com

Word Galaxy Press
467 Saratoga Avenue #602
San Jose, CA 95129

Acknowledgments

My grateful acknowledgments go to the editors of the following publications where these poems, some in earlier versions, first appeared:

Able Muse
    Richard . . . Head . . .

Algebra of Owls
    Spiders . . . Hearted . . .

The American Journal of Poetry
    Beagle . . . Smoking . . .   Passed . . . Died . . .
    Conversation . . . Nation . . .   Purgatory . . . Breeze . . .
    Harambe . . . Wild . . .   Sadism . . . Truth . . .
    Never . . . Again . . .   Trackwalker . . . Track . . .

California Quarterly
    Boulders . . . Dumb . . .   Is . . . Messy . . .

Exit 13
    Chase . . . Place . . .   Lindbergh . . . Kamikaze . . .

Gargoyle
    Against . . . For . . .   Roo-Zuh-Velt . . . History . . .
    Miles . . . Fucker . . .   Secret . . . Life . . .

The HyperTexts
Higgs . . . Pieces . . . Poverty . . . Real . . .

Lighten Up Online
Cargo . . . Knees . . . Monogamy . . . Perforce . . .
Déjà . . . Ensue . . . Parallel . . . Meet . . .
Earwigs . . . Pest . . . Undo . . . Redo . . .

Marin Poetry Center Anthology
Lava . . . Soap . . .

Message in a Bottle
Knock . . . Death . . .

Mind Magazine
Ain't . . . Isn't . . . Razor . . . Splatter . . .
Intelligence . . . Lucidity . . . Waves . . . Particles . . .
Moment . . . Past . . .

Mudlark
Bootsie . . . Truck . . . Lorna . . . Forgotten . . .
Captured . . . Strong . . . Moldenke . . . Castle . . .
Druthers . . . Sleep . . . Propped . . . Down . . .
Force . . . Release . . . Snapping . . . Meat . . .
Hate . . . Like . . . This . . . That . . .
Jumping . . . Down . . . Undergrowth . . . Undertow . . .

Poetalk
Deadline . . . Drown . . .

Raintown Review
Downsizing . . . Unravel . . .

Scene4
    Crush . . . Person . . .   (Parentheses) . . . Fame . . .
    Heroes . . . Ground . . .

Snakeskin
    Aeschylus . . . Instead . . .   Familiarity . . . Contempt . . .
    Cover . . . Song . . .   Time . . . Nasty . . .

Spillway
    Before . . . After . . .   Selfie . . . Here . . .
    Husband . . . Wife . . .   Virtual . . . Technology . . .

Subtle Tea
    Coal . . . Soul . . .   Irony . . . Pollyanna . . .

X-Peri
    Barber . . . White . . .   Namby . . . Pamby . . .
    Boots . . . Slippers . . .   Pardon . . . Me . . .
    Bullshit . . . Horseshit . . .   Puttanesca . . . Respectable . . .
    Burglar . . . Robber . . .   Rappel . . . Climb . . .
    Favorites . . . Loser . . .   Richard . . . Head . . .
    Gesundheit . . . Curse . . .   Thought . . . Cliché . . .
    Guinness . . . Forever . . .   Threw . . . Matter . . .
    Kissing . . . Sad . . .   Virgins . . . 1 . . .
    Mechanical . . . Spontaneity . . .

I am also grateful to Donald Markos, who read and commented on these poems early on, and to friends at Contra Costa Poets for their suggestions and support.

— David Alpaugh

The Double-Title Poem

THE DOUBLE-TITLE POEM has two five-line stanzas. Titles are limited to one word each. The first title reads into the poem or announces its opening motif.

The first word in the second stanza is identical to the first title and is italicized. At least one word in the last two lines of stanza two rhymes with the exit title.

Poems may be metrical or open. If open, lines should be as even in length as possible. End rhyme is to be avoided, but internal rhyme is welcome. Punctuation is inventive, with use of the Emily Dickinson dash to create pauses—and disconnects.

Double-title poems respect both *locality* and *spooky action at a distance*. By treating language as both particle and wave, double-titles aim to provide the aesthetic pleasure of both fixed and open form.

Contents

vi Acknowledgments

ix The Double-Title Poem

3 Before . . . After . . .

4 Favorites . . . Loser . . .

5 Boulders . . . Dumb . . .

6 Coal . . . Soul . . .

7 Harambe . . . Wild . . .

8 Captured . . . Strong . . .

9 Force . . . Release . . .

10 Bootsie . . . Truck . . .

11 Sadism . . . Truth . . .

12 Ain't . . . Isn't . . .

13 Barber . . . White . . .

14 Lorna . . . Forgotten . . .

15 Moment . . . Past . . .

16 Roo-Zuh-Velt! . . . History . . .

17 Boots . . . Slippers . . .

18 Against . . . For . . .

19   Namby . . . Pamby . . .

20   Rappel . . . Climb . . .

21   Propped . . . Down . . .

22   Aeschylus . . . Instead . . .

23   Undergrowth . . . Undertow . . .

24   Earwigs . . . Pest . . .

25   Monogamy . . . Perforce . . .

26   Husband . . . Wife . . .

27   Puttanesca . . . Respectable . . .

28   Kissing . . . Sad . . .

29   Undo . . . Redo . . .

30   Miles . . . Fucker . . .

31   Cover . . . Song . . .

32   Guinness . . . Forever . . .

33   (Parentheses) . . . Fame . . .

34   Selfie . . . Here . . .

35   Virtual . . . Technology . . .

36   Wabi-Sabi . . . Love . . .

37   Hate . . . Like . . .

38   Higgs . . . Pieces . . .

39   Parallel . . . Meet . . .

40   Waves . . . Particles . . .

41   Mechanical . . . Spontaneity . . .

42   Thought . . . Cliché . . .

43   Bullshit . . . Horseshit . . .

44   Is . . . Messy . . .

45   Razor . . . Splatter . . .

46   Lava . . . Soap . . .

47   Cargo . . . Knees . . .

48   Gesundheit . . . Curse . . .

49   Loizeaux . . . Price . . .

50   Never . . . Again . . .

51   Virgins . . . 1 . . .

52   Conversation . . . Nation . . .

53   Poverty . . . Real . . .

54   Burglar . . . Robber . . .

55   Pardon . . . Me . . .

56   Secret . . . Life . . .

57   Intelligence . . . Lucidity . . .

58   Beagle . . . Smoking . . .

59   Wolves . . . Cascade . . .

60   Snapping . . . Meat . . .

61   Spiders . . . Hearted . . .

62   Deadline . . . Drown . . .

63   This . . . That . . .

64   Time . . . Nasty . . .

65   Crush . . . Person . . .

66   Richard . . . Head . . .

67   Heroes . . . Ground . . .

68   Knock . . . Death . . .

69   Druthers . . . Sleep . . .

70   Jumping . . . Down . . .

71   Trackwalker . . . Track . . .

72   Lindbergh . . . Kamikaze . . .

73 Chase . . . Place . . .

74 Moldenke . . . Castle . . .

75 Downsizing . . . Unravel . . .

76 Familiarity . . . Contempt . . .

77 Irony . . . Pollyanna . . .

78 Passed . . . Died . . .

79 Purgatory . . . Breeze . . .

80 Threw . . . Matter . . .

81 Déjà . . . Ensue . . .

83 Notes

Spooky Action at a Distance

The difference between this & that
Depends on where you are
One is always in your face
The other on a star

Before . . .

you popped in here. Lay in a hammock—
sipped Lagavulin; frolicked with your dog
(a Corgi, I believe); danced with the stars;
touched a breast or penis; got skin cancer;
was any Thing behind that scrim you call

Before? Do you remember Fire? Or Ice?
War? Greed? Guilt? Pain? Envy? Wrath?
Did you suffer from insomnia? Wingless
Monkeys *will* call. Greet 'em with laughter.
There's no Wicked Which of the West here

After . . .

Favorites . . .

Parents, teachers encouraged us to pick them.
My favorite color? *Green.* Bird? *Meadowlark.*
(Spotted only in Roger Tory Peterson.) Candy?
Zagnut. (Ruined my teeth.) I was *Teacher's Pet.*
Had a *Best Friend.* Life was all about playing

Favorites. Life continues to be so to this day.
If there isn't any difference between 20 roads,
claim one is your favorite any way! The trick
is to revel in your role as Arbitrary Chooser.
Green is still my favorite color. Red—a sore

Loser . . .

Boulders . . .

ever rattling around in my head. Christ's boulder,
rolled back from the tomb. The one that astonished.
Sisyphus's boulder, which he can't quite roll up to
the top of the hill. The one that hurts. Agates, cat's
eyes, micas, steelies, tumbling out of cloth bags—

Boulders that brought the whole neighborhood out
when a circle was drawn in the dirt. The ones that
delighted. Jesus wielded magic; Sisyphus, muscle;
Howie, Bruce, Doris & me—an opposing thumb.
Exploring the rotundity of marble. All of us struck

Dumb . . .

Coal . . .

My earliest memory—grasping that hard,
black rock in the toe of my stocking, after
the thrill of so many lovely baubles. Dad's
poker-faced grin. Did you get *every*thing?
Back in. Excited. What's *this*? A lump of

Coal! Giver of toys reminding me, Dad said,
that I'd been "just a little bit bad." Suddenly
I saw my *Self*. Like that little girl with a curl
I could be *horrid*. Unto me a Superego was
born. Ignited by a lump of coal. Dad called it

Soul . . .

Harambe . . .

I was 3—& he is *my* earliest memory.
I felt something like love when he put those
big, teddy-bear arms around me. Then adults
screamed, & suddenly I was being dragged
through the water by that 450-pound gorilla,

Harambe. Such fun!—like my big brother,
swirling me around in our swimming pool.
Was I as mistaken as that president who saw
a kindred soul in KGB eyes? No. I was a child.
Didn't know the difference between tame &

Wild . . .

Captured . . .

She was easy to catch. 17, beautiful,
romantic, naive. He'd collected butterflies
as a boy. Wasn't that the best way to secure
a woman? Throw a net over her? Put her in
a BOX where such loveliness would remain

Captured. Trouble was she longed to be free.
Run off, finish high school—maybe even fly
away to college. So our hunter turned farmer.
Punched holes in condoms—till a baby came
along. Then relaxed. His grip unshakably

Strong . . .

Force . . .

Feeding snakes is not fun. I say so, having
done it many times. Ring Necks, DeKays,
Green Snakes refuse to eat in captivity. Pry
their jaws apart gently; ease in a live worm,
slug, cricket or hellgrammite—& may the

Force be with you. Since snakes can go weeks,
even months, without food, before dying, force
feeding isn't something you'll need to do often.
But if your snake spits out proffered orts; if you
long for inner peace; there's only one way to go

Release . . .

Bootsie . . .

Is anything worse than watching your old
dog die? Losing your pup, when you're 6.
A specialist told Mom she was allergic to
dog hair. Dad said, "Sorry. We have to give
him away"—the Cocker Spaniel I named

Bootsie—to a friend of a friend who tried to
turn my pal into a guard dog. *Lord Jesus, let
him break free! Like Lassie, come home to me!*
Jesus tried his best—but ran into Bad Luck.
Bootsie broke out of his pen but was hit by a

Truck . . .

Sadism . . .

On the last day of class, Miss Menafee called
each 4th grader into the coatroom for a private
"chat." When she said that I'd be *staying back*
next year to work on—penmanship—my eyes
began to water. But I was just one victim of her

Sadism that day. She lied to 25 of 26 pupils—
relishing our distress. Till: "Don't cry. You're
not *really* staying back." I wonder about that
boy who had to repeat 4th grade: Andy Booth.
Did Menafee get a kick out of telling *him* the

Truth . . .

Ain't . . .

is a word the South struggled with for years;
trying to shove metaphorical ivory soap into
the mouths of—disenfranchised children. If
only they'd learn to express themselves with
class, their lives might have a little less alas!

Ain't—sworn enemy to upward mobility. Verbal
voodoo so dang hard to shake! Rosa McCauley,
an exception. Rosa seated herself in the first row.
Didn't say *ain't*. Didn't say *'tisn't*. Where Rosa sat
said who she was. Rosa McCauley preferred *is* to

Isn't . . .

Barber . . .

Al's patrons were mostly Irish or Italian immigrants:
fellow graduates of Saint Mary's Elementary. Al cut
hair in a neighborhood that changed color over time
till he became the last Caucasian standing. Suburban
heads remained loyal, driving back in to support their

Barber. Al's crew cuts lasted 6 months, saving my
parents a bundle. Once—while I was being shorn—
a "Negro" poked his head in & asked for a trim.
Al was deferential. Contrite. *My barbering school
didn't teach us how to cut COLORED hair. Only*

White . . .

Lorna . . .

Margolin was our upstairs tenant in Plainfield,
New Jersey. Paid $28 rent which she earned as
a clerk at Macy's. A widow, her only son, Jack,
died in World War II. Though I always said *Mrs.
Margolin*, I'd fetch her mail, so knew her name:

Lorna. Once, when I thought she wasn't looking,
I stuck my tongue out at her. She saw me—& I
had to apologize. "I'm sorry I stuck my tongue
out, Mrs. Margolin." I felt bad then. As this line
gutters, I feel rotten. Outside this poem Lorna is

Forgotten . . .

Moment . . .

The next haiku poet who urges me to seize
it—gets a one-way ticket to Pleasure Island.
There aren't any tongs or clamps or calipers
that can grab & hold that will-o'-the-wisp
for a humongous second, let alone a teentsy

Moment. Take a look at me; be advised that
what you see is not me now, but me some time
ago. A bright star you admire tonight might
already be a black hole. Seize the moment?
No one's ever that fast. Relax & enjoy your

Past . . .

Roo-Zuh-Velt! . . .

Only 9 when Mr. Uhlich—an old man who gave
me 38 pigeons—did me the honor of sharing his
bitterness. I'd seen his shell-shocked son, eyes
cast down, mutter his way about town. 3 sticks of
dynamite exploded from old Mr. Uhlich's mouth:

Roo-Zuh-Velt! "Damn liar promised no mother's
son would die on foreign soil—then let the JAPS
come to get us into war!" I'd yet to get to Honest
Abe. FDR, an utter mystery. But old Mr. Uhlich
& his ruined son were my first brush with *living*

History . . .

Boots . . .

on the ground, out of fashion with the jet set
who prefer to rise, eagle like, to 30,000 feet;
but remain wildly popular on New York City
streets; where Uggs, Trips, & Birkenstocks
prance as the Ball descends on 20-Whatever.

Boots on the ground have arm-chaired warriors,
eager to see leather slogging through hell again.
Nor does sand object to being battered & abused:
like Liza, as 'enry 'iggins wolfs down 'is kippers,
turns 'is back on love & cries, *Fetch my bloody*

Slippers . . .

Against . . .

always makes the scariest face.
Always wields the bloodiest knife.
Strongest crowbar. Bluntest battering ram.
Packs dirty bombs with raspiest nails.
Attaches nuclear warheads to emails.

Against has season tickets to wherever
fans of the status quo gather en masse:
town halls, senate chambers, churches, saloons.
Against is the big bad wolf, howling at the door
to the little lambs within—baa-baa-ing

For . . .

Namby . . .

hesitates to follow a comma into a mute alley
alone—always keeps a bodyguard at his side.
Frequents singles bars, hitting on *An* or *And-y*
to guard against being mugged by declarative
sentences. A verbal coward, yes, but Heeere's

Namby! Too noncommittal for online dating sites
like Zoosk or Christian Mingle—Namby has his
own matchmaker, a wisp of alas, named Hyphen;
who, knowing he's too weak even for a wuss like
Bambi—always hooks him up with his true love

Pamby . . .

Rappel . . .

yourself down the slope of Mount Ever Rest
after being dropped at the summit by a copter.
Who ever heard of an uphill skier? Descent's
sine qua non—where vulnerable skin's aloft.
Vici . . . Vidi . . . Veni. Conquer first. Arrive after.

Rappel yourself down to the Fat Lady's chamber,
million-pound dowry in hand—as Eddie croons
"Oh! My Papa" from the penthouse of a port in air.
See that bloke, halfway down, gathering samphire
to earn a thin dime? Poor sod has just one way to go

Climb . . .

Propped . . .

Up. The whole world by Atlas. Capitalism
by John Galt. Sonny by Cher. Macbeth by
his Lady. Abbott by Costello. Millions by
brassieres & elevator shoes. *Down, down,
I come like glist'ring Phaëton*. No one stays

Propped up. No wonder Mom says stand on
your own two feet & pols urge the poor to
pull themselves up by their own boot straps.
Many crowd Preferment's Gate. Some wear
a crown. You propped up? Prepare to be shot

Down . . .

Aeschylus . . .

sat by the Aegean. Working on a tragedy.
Unaware of the eagle, circling above him.
He had already finished his beginning &
middle; just needed the *peripeteia* to end
(which the eagle held, safe in its beak, for

Aeschylus). Birds know how to break open
a turtle shell to feast on the succulent meat
within. Drop it on a likely rock—from way
up in the sky. Eagle was myopic. Poet, bald.
Turtle smashed the father of tragedy's head

Instead . . .

Undergrowth . . .

makes me shiver. Pulls me towards it—as it
did Robert Frost. *Spooky action at a distance.*
Trees are friendly, willing to be climbed: oak,
maple, birch lead us, with birds, squirrels &
butterflies, to open skies. But what's in the . . .

Undergrowth? Poison ivy, briars, spiders, ants,
scorpions, wasps—& who can forget snakes?
I prefer the simpler dangers of the ocean: peril
I can row. A Great White Attack? More likely
I'll win Lotto—or be swept out to sea by the

Undertow . . .

Earwigs . . .

who are motherless, like neglected children,
lead a tough life (no moms around to feed or
protect them from predators). Women raised
motherless are less attentive to *their* children
than mothered women; & this holds true for

Earwigs. Deprived of maternal love—nymphs
metamorphose into less than exemplary moms.
As *Scientific American* puts it: "Orphaned Bugs
Make Bum Parents." Science humanizing what
I hitherto thought (at best) an ugly & annoying

Pest . . .

Monogamy . . .

Most voles behave like the Duke in *Rigoletto*.
Except—praise be to Darwin—for a laudable
mutation that's faithful *till death do 'em part*.
I could kiss the lab geek who not only found
the chaste gene responsible for such steadfast

Monogamy but messed with libertines' DNA
so they too could taste the joys of married life
(& be as happy as voles can be as prisoners
at a university). Bye, infidelity. Ugly divorce.
Let no vole put asunder what Geneticists join

Perforce . . .

Husband . . .

Hers; & faithful (she thought) for 50 years.
It began with little things: forgetting where he
put his car keys; leaving the teakettle on; later,
asking the same question; seeing Jesus on the
wall; until she heard those dread words: *Your*

Husband has Alzheimer's. After 6 months
in assisted living, he had no idea who she
was, till she caught him in bed with another
inmate, Flo. Old reptile brain sprang to life.
He sat up & shouted: *Oh, my God! It's my*

Wife . . .

Puttanesca . . .

Not created by 5-star chefs, but 50-lira whores
whose *mamma mia*s taught them that the way to
a man's pants is through his nose. That aroma
raised the eyes of many a hungry Napolitano—
to second story windows, offering 2 for 1 delights.

Puttanesca. Olives, garlic, anchovies, capers.
Perfect recipe for busy working girls bent on
cooking up a cheap but savory dish. Easy to
put together on the fly. Still sooo delectable.
Yet, I suspect, even tastier, before it became

Respectable . . .

Kissing . . .

Only 46% of our world cultures enjoy
this phenomenon—the majority bored
or repulsed by oral contact. In Europe,
one-percenters were the innovators, as
kings & queens & courtiers tried

Kissing. Commoners, always eager to ape
the antics of their oppressors, gave it a try;
found it good; & kissing became the fad.
In case you think I'm mad—I read this in
National Geographic. For that 54%, I feel

Sad . . .

Undo . . .

is my favorite function on this word processor.
Allen's *first thought, best thought*—not for me.
I make so many errors (typos, misspellings: *its*
for *it's*; *your* for *you're*) that I thank whatever
software gods may be for my Guardian Angel,

Undo. Had Jobs lived, he might have adapted it
to life itself—devising a button to zap the idiotic
things we do. But be careful what you unscrew.
Let your finger press that button as Dad's sperm
kisses Ma's ovum & skidoo! No one left to press

Redo . . .

Miles . . .

Asked to play piano with the great jazz
trumpeter, I was thrilled. But when I sat
down for our first gig together—you bet
I was plenty nervous. Yes, I was Chick;
& I was good; but, damn it!—He was

Miles. After his solo I riffed my balls off
while he stood by the piano expressionless.
Then just before he raised his horn & his
lips began to pucker—I was in like Flynn
as Miles muttered, *Chick, you're a mother*

Fucker . . .

Cover . . .

I'll write a love song if you cover it for me.
Where would Hoagy's "Stardust" be without
Bing Crosby? Where would eden ahbez be
minus Nat King Cole? I'll gladly supply the
love, joy, grief, wonder. All *you* need do is

Cover. I've attached an MP3 so you can hear
me croak my heart out. (Your voice far more
moving than mine, even without the violins.)
Nobody knows who I am. That's so WRONG.
Cover me. So the world'll know I wrote your

Song . . .

Guinness . . .

I'm sitting here in my underwear with a bottle
of Guinness &—whenever I drink the stuff—
I'm reminded I am not in *The Book of World
Records*. I must do something for the first time
(or better than anyone else) to earn a place in

Guinness. Don't want to down one more hot dog
than X or swim a vast body of water. Need a feat
more sublime than gobbling franks, less stressful
than beating a record. An amazing *Je ne sais quoi*
(whatever). So I can float at the top of a Guinness

Forever . . .

(Parentheses) . . .

(*adalimumab eszopiclone tadalafil rivaroxaban dapagliflozin*). Birth names of panaceas, hyped nightly on TV—skip not lightly off the tongue. No wonder that admen who sell such mouthy monikers—stash them away in alcoves called

Parentheses. (Norma Jeane Mortenson? Frances Gumm? Ilyena Vasilievna Mironov?) Would we adore them half as much had they honored their fathers & mothers? Juliet Capulet asked her Romeo, "What's in a name?" Money, honey, &

Fame . . .

Selfie . . .

Narcissus was the entrepre*newer* who tried
to take one first; but photography being in
its infancy, his underwater camera did him
in. Still, the out-of-focus image that thrilled
Narcissus was our species' first attempt at a

Selfie. Thus began our war on ephemerality
that continues to this day; that Shakespeare
fought with his sonnets; millions via photos
they display. Horton's Who said it for us all,
soft, but clear: *We are here, we are here, we are*

Here . . .

Virtual . . .

reality is icumen in & the real thing doesn't
stand a chance! Caliban's in love with Miranda
till he puts those goggles on. Blonde, brunette,
name your lust—the isle is full of holographs!
Lewd sing *cuccu* & *verteth*—for reality gone

Virtual. So what, if *'Tis new to thee?* Everyone
knows fiction's far more exciting than "reality."
A world elsewhere *is* icumen in; whether brave
or not, it's up to you. Seize Prospero's magic staff,
sans apology. Don't be a Luddite. No one stops

Technology . . .

Wabi-Sabi . . .

This poem is eager to weather . . . decompose
& crumble. Wants the knees on its dungarees
to boast shreds the young find—so beautiful.
I tell this poem to bide its time. Even our most
immortal bard "alteration finds"—thanks to

Wabi-Sabi. Millennials smile as *thespians* cry *verily!*
or *forsooth!* But truth *is* beauty, sun & rain proclaim
as they paint abandoned barns with the rust of nails.
This poem longs to shield 1 word from farther time,
though heartily sick of wedding it to glove or dove:

Love . . .

Hate . . .

This poem promises whips & chains—all the way
down. Blood-curdling scenes of Electra-fying ire
from Medea to Titus Andronicus to Sweeney Todd,
plus real beheadings—on video—with Jihadi John,
segueing into Christ's cheeky slap in the face to

Hate. Too often that word is absurdly hyperbolic.
No way, it lives up to its frown. I hate: *Broccoli?*
Beyoncé? JAY-Z? & so I'm off to Portugal—to
tell Miz Browning we're going on a hunger strike,
demanding she change "How Do I Love Thee" to

Like . . .

Higgs . . .

Thank God, they found that man's boson!
& he, still alive to see it. Well, not *see* it,
exactly, but know it exists inside the Large
Hadron Collider. Talk about the *Decider!*
I apologize for being crass; but without a

Higgs boson you wouldn't have tits, nor would
I have an ass. It's responsible for what Einstein
calls *mass*. Dubbed "The God Particle" because
without it physics can't rule out a deity; with it,
need for such a *deus-ex-machina* thesis falls to

Pieces . . .

Parallel . . .

Universe? I'm *in* 1. & what a hapless
1 it is—for me. I'm trying to be a great
poet. But hardly anyone reads my work.
I've yet to win a Pushcart—let alone a
Pulitzer. Editors couldn't care less if in

Parallel worlds I've won 16 MacArthurs,
9 National Book Awards & a Nobel Prize.
Or that I've been Poet Laureate of Idaho.
Maybe even the Isle of Crete. Small bier.
Because I'm *here*. Parallel Universes never

Meet . . .

Waves . . .

are treated differently by surfers . . . singers . . .
hairdressers. Surfers ride 'em; singers catch
'em; hairdressers, who once said they were
permanent, don't mention 'em at all today.
They can be deadly. Especially ultraviolet

Waves & riptides that sweep swimmers out to sea.
Heisenberg tried to catch undines frolicking within
but was able to grasp nothing but uncertainty. They
ride undulation the same slippery way that meter's
ridden by nouns, verbs, articles. Physicists call 'em

Particles . . .

Mechanical . . .

Engineering springs to mind—then Bergson
on *Le Rire*. What do cockroaches & Malvolio
have in common? *Chitin* makes us laugh or
howl. Put either on a stage & *click-clickety-
clack*—they'll tap-dance the aural essence of

Mechanical. That cosmic Malvolio, Satan,
draws laughter from Milton's God. Dante
ends his *Commedia* with a universal smile.
Risibility can't be repressed, even by Deity.
Heaven & Earth splitting sides at lack of

Spontaneity . . .

Thought . . .

What it did? *Took a shit & ran!* Dead metaphor,
to be sure, but—so pertinent—I wish it were alive.
I love its frank pragmatism. It always takes care of
business before turning tail on whatever comes to
mind. It's so *not* sicklied o'er with the pale cast of

Thought. Had Wittenberg taught Hamlet that saw
instead of Stoicism 101, Fencing 222—Claudius
would die at prayer in 3.3; & Ophelia, Laertes,
Gertrude, Polonius, the sweet Prince himself—all
be alive in 5. Swordplay foiled (*Olé!*) by a rusty

Cliché . . .

Bullshit . . .

Wondering what it is about bulls that led us
to choose *their* excrement to build the most
explosive metaphor in our language? Why
not rat or snake shit? Is El Toro dishonest?
unfair? Are not such epithets themselves—

Bullshit? If the criterion's the size of the turd
wouldn't elephant shit be a far better choice?
Not up for a sniff, but does a bull's shit smell
worse than the crap of other beasts, including
our sapient selves? Worse than first runner-up?

Horseshit . . .

Is . . .

is. You can question it in court to save
your own skin, but although "so much"
depends upon a wheelbarrow—painted
obligatory red—is depends on nothing,
which isn't, but always lies in wait for

Is. Where do *we* fit in? Congenitally unable
to imagine nothing—but knowing at some
future time we will not be—we're on a spit,
turning into *were*. Fire becoming ice. That's
what *is* is. Brrrr! Nothing's pure; but *Esse's*

Messy . . .

Razor . . .

If Occam's right that simplest is best
why such a com-pli-ca-ted universe?
Unseeable holes—light years away—
billions of times larger than the Sun!
Is Physics trying to *blunt* Occam's

Razor? Hey, What-So-Ever! So you want to
lead a Bang? Isn't one Milky Way enough?
Who needs Trillions of Galaxies . . . Parallel
Universes . . . Dark Matter? Jackson Pollock
on a hover board. Goodbye, Occam—Hello

Splatter . . .

Lava . . .

Symbol of the blue-collar muck I left behind
for poetry & the life of the mind: dull gray;
no bouquet. *Gritty*. Meant not for dust & sweat
but for grease & catfish slime. Their ad agency
boasted that the *World's Worst Bath Soap* was

Lava. Nana kept a cake for Grandpa on the sink,
knowing her *Soap of Beautiful Women* had little
to say to a man of Yard & Cellar. Today, still
filthy after scrubbing with *Caress*, I mutter, like
a dope: *What the hell ever happened to Lava*

Soap . . .

Cargo . . .

Pants. My wife has gone to the Lands' End
to buy me 3 pair—black & blue & tan. She
asks me to try them on. I point out that I'm
neither mason, roofer, nor carpenter. Have
neither adze, plane, drill, chisel, caliper. No

Cargo to stash in their holds. You needn't
load tools in 'em, she says. It's just the *style*.
Form trumping content makes me man o' the
people, & buttons keep pickpockets from my
wallet, keys. I'll wear 'em if you *shred* the

Knees . . .

Gesundheit . . .

She doesn't look Aryan. Is she from Berlin?
The woman behind who toasts my "health"
(in German) as I sneeze—waiting in line at
Trader Joe's to check out my wine & cheese.
Later, home, sipping sauvignon—I Google

Gesundheit. Learn how it replaced *God Bless
You* as immigrants increased & faith in deity
declined. I'll bless Mrs. Calabash for toasting
my health when some jerk gives me the finger
or worse. Who doesn't prefer *Gesundheit* to a

Curse . . .

Loizeaux . . .

delivered coal to those who had furnaces &
steam radiators (practically everyone in town).
If coal couldn't be shafted into your bin it had
to be bucketed in at twice the cost. That's how
Mrs. Gorsky had to have *her* coal delivered by

Loizeaux. Whenever Mrs. G. saw Mrs. Stein
she'd hike her skirts & shout, "I shit on you!"
When Loizeaux needed Stein's drive to shaft
in Gorsky's coal, Stein shat back, "No dice!"
In 1943, unusual to see an anti-Semite pay a

Price . . .

Never . . .

If you're old enough to have watched *Shoah*;
maybe even clips of the Nuremberg Trials;
shared Elie Wiesel's *Night*; woke to Celan's
black milk of daylight; wept over *The Diary
of a Young Girl*; then, like me, you promised

Never again! In Aleppo "White Helmets" search
the rubble for moving arms, legs, fingers. *Paris,
London, Brussels, San Bernardino.* Our century's
"rough beast" has no den. Reread Anne's *Diary*.
Still okay to cry. But not to repeat that lie: Never

Again . . .

Virgins . . .

72. No more. No less. "Promise, large promise,"
Johnson says, "is the soul of an advertisement."
At 16, hormones raging, the only female bodies
he'd seen were burkha'd from head to toe. How
provocative those eyes!—HUGE, that promise.

Virgins! In heaven! Unburkha'd! 72 of them!
So he strapped a vest to his own virgin body
& blew himself to bits (with 26 infidels: men,
women, children). 72 virgins? *Caveat emptor!*
Too late. This deal's done. He didn't even get

1 . . .

Conversation . . .

What America needs now? A con-ver-sa-tion!
Everyone yakking about starvation, education,
immigration, sequestration, discrimination,
vaccination, gun regulation, de-cap-i-ta-tion.
Talking Heads! *The Art of the Spiel!* Infinite

Conversation. Chattering incessantly about de-
por-ta-tion . . . de-reg-u-la-tion . . . de-val-u-a-tion
& sundry matters, all ending in *ation.* Can we
earn salvation by talking problems to death?
Can a Tower of Babble save a Blabber-Mouth

Nation . . .

Poverty . . .

So which kind should we prate about? He
who's 70 on the street in a vomity sleeping
bag, clutching a pint of Southern Comfort?
Or a 3-year-old in a hut in Africa, face
covered with flies? Or 1040, IRS-defined

Poverty—with cell phone & big screen TV?
Jesus said, "Leave your junk—& follow me."
Monks pray in cells. Artists paint in garrets.
Damon sings to Chloe from pastoral hillside.
For some, poverty's ideal. For most, savagely

Real . . .

Burglar . . .

There are 2 kinds of thief, I tell my 5-
year-old granddaughter. A robber lets
you know that he wants what's yours
(Rolex, iPad, Barbie doll). Shoves gun
in face & shouts, "Hands-up!" Not so a

Burglar. He knows how to keep a secret.
Sneaks into your room when you're out.
Puts Barbie in pillow case & disappears.
The baseball bat under my bed is there to
clobber a burglar—should he turn into a

Robber . . .

Pardon . . .

Not me!—I'm as guilty of white privilege
as can be! Pardon those with lousy parents,
awful teachers, nasty partners, crummy diets,
shitty music, hooked on opioids & reality TV.
Screwed by Fate (life, a bitch) they deserve a

Pardon more than Mark Rich, Patty Hearst, or
me. I had a loving Mom & Dad, who read me
Tootle the Train: "I think I can . . . I think I can . . ."
be what I want to be. Like Popeye the sailor:
"I am what I am." Don't waste your pardon on

Me . . .

Secret . . .

Tattoo. Inside my armpit. The artist had
to shave my hair before tattooing there.
But I'm swarthy, so once it comes back
thick what's etched in my skin will lurk
like a snake in the forest. My tattooed

Secret. I have a public tattoo on my neck.
$E = mc^2$ breaks the ice with the right sort
of women at singles bars. Still, I'm armed
with 5 words of poetry I'll not share—not
even with a future wife: *I have wasted my*

Life . . .

Intelligence . . .

A flattering abstraction that gives us 2 legs up
on cats, dogs, hyenas & giraffes. 3 cheers
for *Homo sapiens*!!! Hurray for the human race.
Still, let's not be too sanguine about being super
sapient. Clark's Nutcracker, a real contender re

Intelligence. This bird can bury 60,000 pine seeds
in the fall & recall where most of them lie, even
after the earth is covered with snow. If smarter,
why do whales beach themselves? Why do men
fall into the sea? No species boasts monopoly on

Lucidity . . .

Beagle . . .

If Snoopy comes to mind, the image I hope
to replace him with might make you gasp:
a real beagle, strapped in a halter—rubber
mask on forlorn face. Forget Snoopy. Time
to contemplate: the Incredible Puffing

Beagle. Won't ask you to imagine its filthy
lungs or how shreds of that organ ended up
under a microscope. Dogs smoked & died
for mankind. Including those teens on their
break today. Outside Safeway. Joking. &

Smoking . . .

Wolves . . .

Everyone cried: "They're dangerous! bad!"
So I shot one. (It's hanging on my wall.)
So did Pete & Bill & Tom & Phil & Roy
& Dirk & Brad (even Barnaby & Paul)
to keep our wives & children safe from

Wolves. Elk, able to feast with abandon on Aspen
leaves, strip trees bare & when the grass is gone:
starve. Water spreads, evaporates, as river banks
erode. Until, behold! the dry waterfall we, in our
ignorance, made. What do we call this spillway?

Cascade . . .

Snapping . . .

Turtles are quite easy to catch. Aren't all that
dangerous. Pick a big one up by its tail & it
will twirl its head around & try to bite your
hand off—at the wrist. But 2 feet of carapace
will separate your fingers from its jaws, idly

Snapping. Summer, 1951. We caught & kept 5
monsters in a tub in Tommy Oldenhage's yard.
We weren't rich. Snappers don't care what they
eat. We drove Otto, the butcher, crazy, asking
for: 50¢ worth of your very WORST chopped

Meat . . .

Spiders . . .

Desperate for things to say—should you deliver
my eulogy—liken me to Uncle Toby. Instead of
squashing one crawling up a wall—I'd catch it,
open the window, & drop it in our flowerbed.
Please let mourners know I was always kind to

Spiders. & bees. I always helped them out of
our pool when they flew in. I hope you will say
little or nothing about the way I treated people.
Spiders destroy insects. Bees make honey. But
people? Don't get me started! I did *try* to be big-

Hearted . . .

Deadline . . .

Means your branch of the tree's extinct, or you'll
be fired if that ad doesn't reach the *Globe* in time
to appear in Wednesday morning's sports section.
Millions—enslaved to Baudelaire's *dieu sinistre*—
eye the clock on the wall & prepare to meet their

Deadline. Any Midnight. December 31st. Good
Old April 15th. *How much time do I have left,
Doc?* If you know the minute, hour, day, week,
year you can plan ahead. But deadlines are hard
to pin down. You may be hit by a bus today—or

Drown . . .

This . . .

is here & now. Today. The gas & electric bill
you'd better pay. Pain in your side—that will
not go away. Why let a fork (or 2) in the road
leave you forever glum? Sperm kisses ovum.
Ultrasound. (You are going to have—a son.)

This is forever in your face—Duke of the
Dotted Line. Free Granny Glasses at every
polling place. THINK, *Lucky! Concentrate!*
This ain't over till it's over; till *sit* becomes
sat; bats return to their caves—& that's

That . . .

Time . . .

hangs heavy on our hands once it stops flying.
Waits for no man, but halts in the middle of the
road for Elizabeth Bishop's moose. All agree:
Time is Money in disguise; but when it comes
to how much an hour's worth—we differ big

Time. In Seattle, 15 dollars. In Harare, 50 cents.
In Washington, DC, 114 million on US national
debt. The good news? Andy's Wingèd Chariot
has our back! Father T so vast he heals—ALL
(although we do our best to kill 'im when 'e's)

Nasty . . .

Crush . . .

A Scary Insect. The name of the video game
I hope to make 10 million bucks on. I lure you
into my Application, promising free play. You
rack up thousands of points—zapping ant, bee,
gnat. Thrill to the *splat* that punctuates each

Crush. Once hooked (for a modest fee) match
your dexterity against increasingly nasty pests,
flitting about on your screen. (Ever try to swat
a tsetse fly?) Delight in Mayhem may abate or
worsen when you graduate to Crush A Scary

Person . . .

Richard . . .

Cory. I'm the doc who diagnosed his cancer;
told Dick he had 6 months to live. 5 minutes
later, he was with his lawyer, drawing up the
will in which he'd give: the royal riches you
so envied to Red Cross & Salvation Army.

Richard Cory. Dead Man Walking. Fooled folks
on the pavement. Not me. When the pain finally
got so bad he couldn't walk downtown; couldn't
even climb out of bed—doctor, friend, I slipped
Dick the gun he used to put a bullet through his

Head . . .

Heroes . . .

We love to see them fall. Thetis left a
smidge of mortality on Achilles' heel,
knowing we'd tire of Eternal Triumph.
Strolling to Calvary, most tickled to see
Iron Nails Run In—to the Greatest of

Heroes (mankind cannot bear very much
Divinity). As for superstars, worshipped
from afar; though we clap till our palms
are sore, we're not wholly displeased by
the sound—when one of them hits the

Ground . . .

Knock . . .

yourself out! Daring death, as young as nine or
ten, we'd inhale good old New Jersey air again
& again until, minds spinning, we'd collapse
onto couch or floor. Far headier than all those
deadly juvenile jokes that began with a *Knock*

Knock, followed by that obligatory *Who's there?*
I tap my skull & pose that question, more now
than ever before (as I grope for the name of this
or that star I saw last night on TV). Knock your
self out, kid. Take a deep breath. "Who's there?"

Death . . .

Druthers . . .

I want that sudden, explosive pain in my temple
or that sharp tightening of right or left ventricle.
Though I don't *prefer* it, I'm okay with swerving
to avoid a chipmunk & plunging over a 50-foot
embankment. As I'd like it—if I get to have my

Druthers. I found Dad—eyes closed—peaceful
in his easy chair. Isn't that the ideal way to go?
Hell, no!—I want to *know* I'm dying. But God
has a dark sense of humor. Can be a real creep.
May be planning to squash me like a bug in my

Sleep . . .

Jumping . . .

up & down up & down up & down up & down
with Miley or Jay-Z. Feet more often in the air
than on the ground. Mouths twerking "That's
America to Me." No "Skylark" in Cheap Thrill
Park: bumping, dumping, humping, thumping,

Jumping. 6 teenyboppers boom box onto BART.
Somersault on hand rails! Break dance the aisle!
I toss 50¢ into their tip hat, while Ella murmurs
"Skylark" on my noise-cancelling earphones—
& the world jumps up & down up & down up &

Down . . .

Trackwalker . . .

You go down into the subway after midnight
when there's nobody on the platform . . . ease
yourself onto the tracks . . . enter the dimly lit
tunnel, under the sleeping city, well aware of
what'll happen should you touch that third rail.

Trackwalker. Your woods. Your "Acquainted
with the Night." Your *danger* (a tad too young
to fight our last war). Thrilling to feel the rails
shake. See that light up ahead. Will blind luck
have your back—as you leap to the opposite

Track . . .

Lindbergh . . .

Charles, caused me much grief—in Maui, on
the road to Hana. Quite a skinny road—so if
you're afraid of heights, you may want to go
snorkeling instead. Who knew the flyer lived
on Maui—till our bus stopped at the grave of

Lindbergh. As I walked to the site, a bee buzzed
my head—so I brushed it away. It flew back up,
dove down, & stung my arm. I was ill for days.
The bee (apiarists assure me) died. So, though I
don't think Lindy was a Nazi, my attacker *was* a

Kamikaze . . .

Chase . . .

No way we'll catch the sun. Our planet spinning
faster than Southwest can fly us back to Oakland.
Darkness will fall before we arrive. Still, clouds
have yet to redden, & it's a real hoot to root for
our Red Baron pilot—no matter how quixotic his

Chase. 6 miles high—I feel like the poet in "You,
Andrew Marvell," catching light's disappearing act
(although Archie didn't wear Bluetooth earbuds).
Fly. Ever so fast. Not even falcons win this race.
As Heifetz plays "Clair de lune," I lose it in a lofty

Place . . .

Moldenke . . .

was a doctor—but not the kind who stuck
a thermometer up your behind. No. He had
something called a "PhD." Knew all about
"Metallurgy." He came to Jefferson School
to lecture, mostly about gold & silver, did

Moldenke. Once we visited the replication of
his family estate in Denmark. Gawking at its
turrets, cannons, armored suits—I intuited the
meaning of *vassal.* I lived in what mom called
Home Sweet Home—but Moldenke lived in a

Castle . . .

Downsizing . . .

is on our minds more & more these days.
I'm tired of plucking weeds & cleaning
gutters. Our nest long empty, why do we
need 5 bedrooms? 1, Donne says, is
a veritable *everywhere*. Surely we can bear

Downsizing to 3. A den for you, a den
for me—*as to the bed's feet, life is shrunk*.
No mortgage payment—plenty of cash for
travel. So why did we spring for this plush
Persian rug? Maybe we're not yet ready to

Unravel . . .

Familiarity . . .

is at its best when you return after 2 years
at sea; enter your shanty & there's your bed . . .
your desk . . . your ceiling . . . floor. You even feel
fondness for that awful "art work" on the wall.
You sit on the porch with your mate. Revel in

Familiarity. Sharing the same bed—for 50 years.
Visiting haunts together an umpteenth time. Dining
at a favorite inn. Ordering the dish you always do.
As for that Big Bad Wolf cliché? You're exempt.
Familiarity can just as well breed Love & Joy as

Contempt . . .

Irony . . .

I remember Ida saying she didn't care for it—
when it meant the world to me. Youth's go-to
ammo against confusion, alienation, suffering,
engagement, love. Voltaire in hand, put on a
smirky face—& slay all your dragons with

Irony. Rereading "To Autumn" (Ida long gone)
I'm autumnal now & 90% irony free.
Keats's "mellow fruitfulness . . . gathering swallows."
Ripeness to the core. *Manna*. But I always wash
it down with a jigger of Swift to give the finger to

Pollyanna . . .

Passed . . .

I'm about to send one of those shattering
emails. A mutual friend has *passed away*.
But isn't that a smiley-faced euphemism
for what brain cancer did to Jim? Lucky
him, off on a holiday cruise or excursion.

Passed. Like a ship in the night. Now with
bikinied babes on the Riviera or zip-lining
Kauai! A knockout word for what occurred
spars with my rope-a-dope attempt to hide
the bell-ringing fact: another old friend has

Died . . .

Purgatory . . .

(Schopenhauer suggests) isn't just a bad
dream in Dante's mind—or terror firma
south of Hades. This is *it*, pal. Saint Peter
searched your soul; pointed his piscatory
finger towards birth; &, yes, you are in

Purgatory. Earth's a far cry from Hell.
Why bitch, as you expiate this & that?
Be you short, lovelorn, impoverished,
flat-chested, dying from Lou Gehrig's
disease. Next to the Ninth Circle, life's a

Breeze . . .

Threw . . .

a slew of poems down an elliptical staircase.
Picked 'em up, willy-nilly, to baptize my muse
in the blood of random order. Dame Fortune
puts this poem on page 80. I'd've put it on page 22.
Unintended consequences happened when I

Threw. All I meant to do was slay the *Decider*.
But, choral director gone, can there be a choir?
Drifting down your stare, with chaos in the air,
go my snake eyes—&, like dice, they scatter.
I'm threw. What say you? Do chance thoughts

Matter . . .

Déjà . . .

If you get the eerie feeling that you've read this before—re that slow-ball Yogi Berra calls *Déjà Vu*—it may be that Nietzsche, Schopenhauer, & a few wacko physicists are right! that there's a recurring universe (or 2). So why be surprised when feeling

Déjà Vu? Big Bang! Expansion. After skillions of light years—Big Crunch! Singularity. Then? Bang! All over again. So, if cosmological constants hold true, you've read these lines an infinite number of times before. What's more—infinite readings will

Ensue . . .

Notes

"Favorites . . . Loser . . ." on page 4: Roger Tory Peterson's *A Field Guide to the Birds of Eastern and Central North America* (first edition, 1934) was biblical for birdwatchers when I was growing up as one.

"Harambe . . . Wild . . ." on page 7: On May 28, 2016, keepers at the Cincinnati zoo shot and killed a gorilla named Harambe, after a three-year-old boy wandered into its enclosure. On June 16, 2001, George W. Bush found Vladimir Putin *trustworthy* because: "I looked the man in the eye. I was able to get a sense of his soul."

"Ain't . . . Isn't . . ." on page 12: McCauley was Rosa Parks's maiden name.

"Roo-Zuh-Velt! . . . History . . ." on page 16: Pearl Harbor conspiracy buffs imagine that government officials, including President Roosevelt, had advance knowledge of Japan's attack on Pearl Harbor and let the planes come to justify getting into the war.

"Boots . . . Slippers . . ." on page 17: "Slogging through hell" is an allusion to Yip Harburg's 1931 "Brother, Can You Spare a Dime," originally sung by Bing Crosby and Rudy Vallee: "Half a million boots went sloggin' through hell/ And I was the kid with the drum."

"Rappel . . . Climb . . ." on page 20: *Vici . . .Vidi . . . Veni* reverses Caesar's famous I came, I saw, I conquered. Eddie is, of course, Eddie Fisher, who had the hit song, "Oh! My Papa" in 1953. The "port in air" Fisher sings from sounds suspiciously like the one mentioned by Wallace Stevens in his "Anecdote of a Jar." In *King Lear* (Act 4, Scene 6), the blinded Gloucester thinks he's at the edge of Dover Cliff, thanks to his son Edgar's marvelous description of the dizzying descent: "Halfway down/ Hangs one that gathers samphire; dreadful trade!"

"Propped . . . Down . . ." on page 21: John Galt is the hero of Ayn Rand's *Atlas Shrugged*. "Down, down, I come; like glist'ring Phaëton/ Wanting the manage of unruly jades" (Richard II, Act 3, Scene 3). "Unnumber'd suppliants crowd Preferment's gate / Athirst for wealth, and burning to be great" (Samuel Johnson, "The Vanity of Human Wishes").

"Undergrowth . . . Undertow . . ." on page 23: Robert Frost's attraction to "undergrowth" is most evident in "Into My Own," "Come In," and "The Road Not Taken."

"Earwigs . . . Pests . . ." on page 24: "Orphaned Bugs Make Bum Parents" appeared in *Scientific American*, April 2016.

"Monogamy . . . Perforce . . ." on page 25: The research for the vole experiment is described by Yuval Harari in *Sapiens: A Brief History of Humankind*.

"Kissing . . . Sad . . ." on page 28: "A Kiss Isn't Just a Kiss," *National Geographic*, February 2016.

"Miles . . . Fucker . . ." on page 30: My versification of an anecdote told by Chick Corea at the Masonic Auditorium in San Francisco in 1978. Chick called Miles's metaphor the greatest compliment he ever received on his playing.

"Cover . . . Song . . ." on page 31: In 1948, Nat King Cole sang eden ahbez's only hit "Nature Boy" (subsequently *covered* by scores of singers). Barry Manilow covered Bruce Johnston's "I Write the Songs the Whole World Sings" which reached number one on *Billboard* in 1976.

"(Parentheses) . . . Fame . . ." on page 33: With a clear preference for the amphibrachal foot, admen replace scientific tongue twisters with HuMIRa, LuNESta, CiALis, XaRELto, FarXIga, and scores of other prescription drugs. Replacing birth names has been most profitable for Judy Garland, Marilyn Monroe, Helen Mirren, and other celebrities.

"Selfie . . . Here . . ." on page 34: The mispronunciation of *entrepreneur* is almost universal among TV blatherers. For those who don't have children or grandchildren the quotation in the last line of this poem is from Dr. Seuss's *Horton Hears a Who*.

"Virtual . . . Technology . . ." on page 35: Scholarly opinion is split as to the meaning of "verteth" in the popular middle English lyric "Sumer is icumen in." Is the buck *farting*? or—*vert* meaning *green* in French—hiding in the foliage? Other allusions are to *The Tempest*.

"Wabi-Sabi . . . Love . . ." on page 36: Wabi-Sabi is the traditional Japanese aesthetic that finds beauty in things imperfect, impermanent, and incomplete—things that have been fondled by Time. Regarding the vulnerability of words, Dr. Johnson notes: "Though art may sometimes prolong their duration, it will rarely give them perpetuity; and their changes will be almost always informing us, that language is the work of man, of a being from whom permanence and stability cannot be derived."

"Hate . . . Like . . ." on page 37: "Jihadi John" produced ISIS videos showing beheadings of more than twenty captives, including humanitarian aid workers. He was killed by a drone strike in 2015. "How Do I Love Thee" is the most famous poem in Elizabeth Browning's *Sonnets from the Portuguese* (our poet was off to Portugal to chasten her diction).

"Higgs . . . Pieces . . ." on page 38: In the sixties physicist Peter Higgs theorized that there must be a particle responsible for mass. He was proven right in 2012 when his boson was detected inside the Large Hadron Collider on the border between France and Switzerland.

"Waves . . . Particles . . ." on page 40: Undines, first named in the alchemical writings of Paracelsus, are elemental beings associated with water. Their name is derived from the Latin word *unda*, meaning waves.

"Mechanical . . . Spontaneity . . ." on page 41: In *Le Rire*, Henri Bergson asks why we laugh and answers that we do so whenever we perceive humans acting *mechanically*.

"Thought . . . Cliché . . ." on page 42: When I was growing up and unable to make a decision on a usually trivial matter, my mother would rocket me into action with the folk question "What did Thought do?" and her answer: "Took a shit and ran!" I knew it was time for me to "get off the pot" (to ply another dead metaphor) and make a decision. Mine were a lot easier to make than Prince Hamlet's.

"Bullshit . . . Horseshit . . ." on page 43: The *Oxford English Dictionary* cites T. S. Eliot as first to leave a *written* record of the word in his poem "The Triumph of Bullshit."

"Is . . . Messy . . ." on page 44: This poem was inspired by Jim Holt's *Why Does the World Exist* where he asks: "Why is there something rather than nothing?"

"Lava . . . Soap . . ." on page 46: A fan of radio's Helen Trent, Nana was loyal to Helen's sponsor, "Camay, the soap of beautiful women."

"Gesundheit . . . Curse . . ." on page 48: Comedian Jimmy Durante always signed off with: "Good night, Mrs. Calabash, wherever you are."

"Secret . . . Life . . ." on page 56: The speaker has had the last line of James Wright's poem "Lying in a Hammock at William Duffy's Farm in Pine Island, Minnesota" tattooed into his armpit (ouch!). Wright's line is itself an allusion to the last line of Rainer Maria Rilke's "Archaic Torso of Apollo" (widely translated as "You must change your life").

"Beagle . . . Smoking . . ." on page 58: In 1970, Dr. Oscar Auerbach upset the tobacco industry by announcing that twenty of the eighty-six beagles he had "trained" to smoke had developed cancers.

"Spiders . . . Hearted . . ." on page 61: As Uncle Toby releases a fly that has been tormenting him in *Tristram Shandy*, he says: "Why should I hurt thee?—This world surely is wide enough to hold both thee and me."

"Deadline . . . Drown . . ." on page 62: The clock in line four is Baudelaire's "L'Horloge," which he personifies as a sinister, frightening, implacable god ("*Horloge! dieu sinistre, effrayant, impassible*").

"This . . . That . . ." on page 63: Lucky is the baggage-carrying intellectual in Beckett's *Waiting for Godot* who delivers an astonishing monologue.

"Time . . . Nasty . . ." on page 64: In Elizabeth Bishop's "The Moose," a Boston-bound bus stops with a jolt as a "grand, otherworldly" animal appears "on the moonlit macadam," "taking its time." "Andy" is, of course, Andrew Marvell, who has "Time's wingèd chariot" ever at his back.

"Richard . . . Head . . ." on page 66: Now that we know that Richard Cory's physician helped him commit suicide, we can't help but wonder if he might not be the same doctor on trial for euthanizing another patient by lethal injection in Edwin Arlington Robinson's "How Annandale Went Out."

"Trackwalker . . . Track . . ." on page 71: This poem is in memory of Boo Shepherd—a teenager I knew in the early sixties. None of Boo's friends were aware that he was a trackwalker. One night, in a New York City subway tunnel, Boo jumped onto the opposite track to avoid an oncoming train and was killed by a train coming the other way. Frost's sonnet "Acquainted with the Night" is also about lonely, eerie late-night walking.

86

"Chase . . . Place . . ." on page 73: The "You, Andrew Marvell" poet is Archibald MacLeish: "And here face down beneath the sun/ And here upon earth's noonward height/ To feel the always coming on/ The always rising of the night."

"Moldenke . . . Castle . . ." on page 74: Several dozen castles were built in New Jersey in the early part of the twentieth century by immigrants who became wealthy enough to replicate family abodes in "the old country." The Moldenke Castle, in Watchung, New Jersey, was one of these.

"Downsizing . . . Unravel" on page 75: In "The Good Morrow," John Donne explains to his mistress that love "makes one little room an everywhere"; but in the diminished world of "A Nocturnal upon Saint Lucy's Day" "the sun is spent," "the world's whole sap is sunk," and "as to the bed's feet, life is shrunk."

"Irony . . . Pollyanna . . ." on page 77: The notion that our poet is "ninety percent irony free" should be taken *cum grano salis.*

"Purgatory . . . Breeze . . ." on page 79: Schopenhauer writes: "If, consequently, you should ask the propounders of [Brahmanism and Buddhism] where and what all those who have not attained to redemption are, they would reply: 'Look around you: here is where they are, this is what they are: this is their arena, this Sansara, i.e., the world of desire, of birth, of pain, of age, of sickness and of death.' . . . It is a sufficiently evil place: it is Purgatory. . . ."

"Threw . . . Matter" on page 80: Here, William S. Burrough's "cut-up technique" is carried to an extreme. The novelist at least retained partial control over *his* arrangements when he snipped his text into sections and then put them together in different sequences. Our poet puts himself at the mercy of Dame Fortune. Since what this poet says does not comport with the actual order of the poems, he appears to be speaking from a parallel universe. Or is he the book's black hole?

"Déjà . . . Ensue . . ." on page 81: "It's déjà vu all over again" is one of Berra's famous "Yogi-isms." Another ("When you come to a fork in the road, take it") is glanced at in "Favorites . . . Loser . . ." on page 4.

DAVID ALPAUGH still thinks of himself as a Jersey boy but has lived long enough in the San Francisco Bay Area to be included in the Heyday Press anthology, *California Poetry from the Gold Rush to the Present*, and to have been a finalist for Poet Laureate of California. He holds degrees in English from Rutgers University and the University of California, Berkeley, where he was both a Woodrow Wilson and Ford Foundation Fellow. His poems have appeared in more than a hundred literary journals from *Able Muse* to *Poetry* to *ZYZZYVA*, and his first collection, *Counterpoint*, won the Nicholas Roerich Poetry Prize from Story Line Press. David Alpaugh's essays, "The Professionalization of Poetry" (*Poets & Writers Magazine*), "What's *Really* Wrong With Poetry Book Contests" (*Rattle*), and "The New Math of Poetry" (*Chronicle of Higher Education*)—have been widely discussed online. His musical play, *Yesteryear: 3 Days in Paris with François Villon*, was recently published by *Scene4*. Since he debuted the double-title poem in *Mudlark* in 2016, more than a hundred have appeared in journals and anthologies. He currently teaches literature for the Osher Lifelong Learning Institute (OLLI) at their UC Berkeley and Cal State East Bay campuses.

www.ingramcontent.com/pod-product-compliance
Lightning Source LLC
Chambersburg PA
CBHW021407090426
42742CB00009B/1052